SAINT CATHERINE
OF SIENA

CONTENTS

SAINT CATHERINE
OF SIENA

CHAPTER 1

SAINTS IN THE SKY

THERE WAS once a good man named Jacopo, who made a living at a strange business. He was a dyer, that is, he took cloths of plain colors and turned them into all the shades of the rainbow. When rich people saw Jacopo's purple silk, his scarlets and blues and yellows, they usually decided on some new clothes right away and bought yards and yards of the wonderful material. In such a way Jacopo became quite wealthy and built a nice house for his wife and family.

Now, Jacopo's house was a big place. In it lived Jacopo's numerous children, his wife, his servants and the men and boys who helped around the shop and sold goods to customers. Very seldom was there a quiet moment in Jacopo's house. Something was always going on, either a banquet, a business deal, a wedding or a visit from the neighbors. There was always food cooking in the kitchen, too, for it took a lot to feed all the people who lived with Jacopo or who came to visit him. It was a busy place, Jacopo's house. His children loved it, and when any

1

of the sons got married they always brought their brides home to live. In fact, as years went by, Jacopo's house became more and more crowded, so that one wondered how it could ever hold any more people.

One day in the year 1347 Jacopo and his wife Lapa, who lived in the Italian city of Siena and already had twenty-three children, were blessed by God with twin baby girls.

"Goodness!" cried the neighbors. "Where will they put any more children?"

"There was never a house like Jacopo's house," said the relations. "They will find room somehow."

And Jacopo and Lapa did, although as it turned out only one of the new little girls lived. They named her Catherine.

"I hope she grows up to be beautiful!" sighed Jacopo's wife. "Then she can marry a rich man and we can enlarge the shop."

Jacopo nodded. "Her hair is the color of red gold," he said dreamily. As he looked at his little daughter in her cradle, he began to think of making up a new color for some new silks which had just come in from the East.

Catherine grew up in her father's big house, amid all the noise and clatter of so many people. It was easy to see she would never be beautiful. Only her golden hair set her apart from other little girls in the town. It was really lovely, so long and soft and curly.

"Will you stand still?" cried her mother one morning, as she tried to comb the pretty locks. "Why are you so fidgety?"

"Because I hate having my hair fixed," said the little girl. "I want to go out and play in the yard."

"Well, you can't play in the yard," said her mother. "I have a package I want taken to your sister Bonaventura. And I want you to look nice when you go to her house. So stand still and let me fix you."

Catherine's brown eyes shone. Bonaventura, her favorite sister, was married and lived not far away. It was always such fun to go and see her because Bonaventura understood that little girls liked presents. And good things to eat.

"Can I go alone, Mother?" she cried. "It would be so nice to go visiting by myself just for once!"

"Nonsense!" cried her mother, who was suddenly remembering that twelve people were coming to dinner. "Your brother Stefano will go with you. And remember—go straight to Bonaventura's. No stopping to play on the way, or to visit in church. You are too young to be out by yourselves for long."

"But I am six years old," Catherine started to say, then changed her mind. Company for dinner always upset her mother, who was inclined to be cross on such days.

Soon Catherine and Stefano, who was a bit older, were on their way to their married sister's house. The sun was shining brightly. The streets were crowded with people. Ox carts jolted up and down. A group of wandering musicians had stopped to play and sing near the great fountain in the square.

"Oh, let's listen to them!" cried Stefano, running

ahead. "They have a dancing bear and a monkey!"

But Catherine remembered her mother's words and shook her head.

"No, we must go straight to Bonaventura's," she said, and took Stefano's hand firmly in hers.

They stayed at Bonaventura's house for an hour only, and then started home with a package for their mother. This time they did not come through the crowded streets of the town but took a short cut through an open field. There were many flowers growing along the way, and Catherine and Stefano picked a few as they walked along. Back of the Dominican church, which stood over towards the town, they were even more plentiful.

"Let's go and get some daisies," said Stefano. "There are loads of them over near the church."

"Mother said to come right back . . ." said Catherine, and then suddenly her heart skipped a beat.

Above the Dominican church, right in the middle of the blue sky, right above the fields of white daisies, were people. They were standing in the sky as though it were the most natural thing to do, and some were kneeling before a great white throne. A King was seated on the throne, and He seemed pleased with the people about Him. He even seemed pleased with Catherine, for He turned in her direction and smiled at her.

"Oh!" cried the little girl, falling to her knees. "How beautiful it all is!"

Stefano stared. "What's the matter?" he cried. "What are you kneeling down for?"

"NO, WE MUST GO STRAIGHT TO BONAVENTURA'S."

But Catherine did not hear. Her eyes were fixed on the sky, on the wonderful people in shining robes, on the King. She knew, without being told, that the King was really Our Lord, and when He raised His Hand to bless her, she could hardly believe it.

Stefano looked at the blue sky over the church, but there was nothing there except a white cloud, a very ordinary cloud. Certainly that was nothing to make Catherine's face so happy, to cause her to kneel down in the field as though she were praying.

"What is the matter with you?" he asked. "Mother will be cross if we are late with this parcel."

And then, since Catherine still did not answer, he began to be angry.

"Will—you—come—on?" he said.

Awakened from her vision, Catherine turned to Stefano, and her eyes were shining.

"Oh, if you could see what I see, you would not bother me! Look, Stefano, at the wonderful people in the air! They are saints, I am sure. And that is Our Lord, sitting on the throne and smiling at us."

Stefano looked to where Catherine pointed. "Silly!" he laughed. "There are no people in the air. How could there be? And Our Lord is in the church, not over it. You know that."

Catherine's smile faded. Even as Stefano was speaking she saw that the wonderful vision had gone. There were no longer any saints in the sky. And Our Lord was gone, too.

"Well, are you coming?"

HER EYES WERE FIXED ON THE SKY,
ON THE WONDERFUL PEOPLE IN SHINING ROBES.

Catherine nodded. "I'm coming," she said, but her heart was sad. The saints and Our Lord had been so beautiful. Now the sky seemed empty without them.

"You shouldn't make up stories and tell them as though they were true," Stefano said presently. "It isn't right."

"But I didn't make up a story!" replied Catherine quickly. "There were saints in the sky, Stefano. And I could have been looking at them yet, if you hadn't bothered me."

The little boy shrugged his shoulders. What could you do with girls? They talked and talked and always wanted to be in the right. They would never admit they could make a mistake.

There was a great deal of confusion in Jacopo's house as the two children neared the gate. Strange bearded men, whom they knew to be cloth merchants from the East, were standing in the courtyard. Piled high in the workrooms were great bales of silk and wool. Vats of dye simmered on the fire and young men stood over them, stirring them with large wooden ladles. It was a busy day for Jacopo, the dyer.

"There's my cat!" cried Stefano. "Let's make a daisy chain for her neck with these flowers!"

But Catherine shook her head. She was thinking about the strange people in the sky over the Dominican church, the strange people who must be saints. She was sure one of them had been Saint John, the cousin of Our Lord, and two others, Saint Peter and Saint Paul. There were pictures of these

STRANGE BEARDED MEN,
CLOTH MERCHANTS FROM THE EAST,
WERE STANDING IN THE COURTYARD.

great men all through the town. But why had they been in the sky? And why had she, a little girl, seen them?

"I never saw a saint before," she thought. "They seemed awfully nice."

And then an idea came into Catherine's head, as she stook watching Stefano playing with his cat. Why couldn't she be a saint, too? Why couldn't she be holy and love Our Lord as Saint Peter and Saint Paul and Saint John had loved Him? Why couldn't she be up in the sky over the Dominican church, and very close to Our Lord on His throne?

"I guess I couldn't be a saint at home," she said. "There is too much noise and there are too many people. But if I could go away. . . if I could have a nice quiet place where Our Lord could tell me how to be good. . ."

"Catherine!" called a woman's voice suddenly. "Come here at once!"

Recognizing her mother's voice, Catherine went into the house. Her golden curls were tangled from the wind and would have to be combed again. Her hands were dirty from picking flowers. But what did anything matter? She had seen a vision. She had seen a most wonderful vision in the sky. And soon she would be a saint, too, a saint with wonderful shiny robes like Saint Peter and Saint Paul and Saint John.

CHAPTER 2

THE LITTLE HERMIT

CATHERINE HAD heard about hermits. They were people who lived in caves, far away from the noise and bustle of the town, and they spent all their time in thinking about God. Saint John the Baptist had been a hermit for many years. Saint Anthony of Egypt had been another, and Saint Paul and Saint Romuald and even Saint Mary Magdalen.

"Perhaps if I were a hermit, too, I should see Our Lord again," Catherine told herself. "Our Lord loves hermits, I am sure. He makes saints out of them."

So, with a fast-beating heart, Catherine decided to be a hermit and go away from her father's big house and all her brothers and sisters. Early one morning she crept down to the kitchen, for she would need some food and drink for the journey. It would be quite a little walk to the wild country outside the town. Perhaps she would even find some other hermits there already.

"Oh, but I must hurry!" she thought. "No one

must suspect anything!" And seizing a loaf of bread and small jug of water, she ran silently into the courtyard. Stefano's cat lifted a sleepy head as she went by, and for a moment Catherine felt a little lonely. How fine it would be if her brother were coming, too! It would be so nice if they both could be holy hermits and see saints in the sky together.

"But a hermit must live alone," said Catherine to herself. "Goodbye, Stefano. I shall pray for you every day, and for all my other friends and relations." Then, not stopping to look again at the sleepy grey cat on the steps of her father's shop, she went quickly through the courtyard and out into the cobbled street.

Catherine had started her trip to the wilderness before the sun was up. Presently the warm rays began to streak over the hills. The sky turned from pale grey to gold and red. Soon it was a bright and lovely blue. Birds sang in the trees. As time went by, Catherine noted that the houses were becoming farther and farther apart. She had been walking for several hours and probably would soon reach the wilderness. The country was growing wilder and stranger and it had been a long time since she had seen a farmer with his market cart or a peddler with his wares.

"I am miles and miles away from home now," the little traveler told herself. "And I shall never go back, because I can love God best when there is no one around. Oh, but I do hope Father will not try to find me and bring me home again!"

As she was thinking about the possibility of her

"I AM MILES AND MILES AWAY FROM HOME."

family setting out to look for her, Catherine gave a cry of joy. Right before her, just at the turn of the winding path, was a cave—the very sort of cave meant for hermits. Truly, it was the prettiest cave possible, almost hidden from view by the vines and bushes growing about it.

"Thank You, dear God, for letting me find this beautiful cave!" cried Catherine. "Here I will live for the rest of my days, and never love anyone but You!"

Then, pushing her way through the tangle of bushes, Catherine went up to the cave and looked inside. It was cool here; the sun could not strike through the thick rock, and the green vines made a sort of curtain over the entrance. There was not a sound to be heard, save the chirping of the birds and the murmur of a little brook that was close by. It was truly a peaceful spot, well hidden from view, and the very place for a hermit. Catherine knelt down on the ground and was very happy. Her trip had certainly turned out well.

Later in the day a strange thing happened to the new hermit. She had been kneeling in prayer for some time, on the rough floor of the cave, when suddenly she felt herself moving gently upward. She was not afraid to find herself floating in the air, only a little puzzled. Presently a voice said to her:

"Do you love Me, Catherine?"

It was Our Lord's voice, although how it was that she knew this, Catherine could not tell. But she was full of joy to think that at last she was hearing from Him.

"I love You more than myself, more than anyone or anything!" cried the little girl. "Only may I see You, please?"

It was growing dark in the cave, and Catherine's eyes searched the empty space from which the voice seemed to come. But she could make out nothing. Not this time the beautiful vision which she had seen above St. Dominic's church back home, with crowds of shining figures and Our Lord on a great white throne. This time there was nothing at all.

But then the strange and beautiful voice spoke again.

"You want to be a hermit, Catherine?"

"Oh, yes, dearest Lord, so that I may spend all my time in thinking about You!"

"Then you love Me very much and will do anything I ask?"

"Anything, dearest Lord, no matter how hard it is!"

"Then return to your home, little one. I call others to be hermits in a cave, but not you."

Return home! Others to be hermits, not she! Catherine's eyes filled with tears.

"But, dearest Lord, I want to be a saint!" she cried. "I want to think of You all the time. I cannot do that at home."

The kindly voice replied, "Yes, you can. That will be your life's work: to live in the world and bring others to Me. Priests and nuns and hermits are My good servants, but I have need of saints in families, too. What is your answer?"

"Yes, dear Lord," said Catherine humbly, and, as she spoke, she felt herself floating down to the floor of the cave. Her day of being a hermit was over. Our Lord had other work for her to do. Now she must make haste to return to the busy town.

As she picked up her water jug and the remains of her loaf of bread, a dreadful thought crossed her mind. How angry her mother would be when she returned home! There would be questions from everyone. Where had she been all day? Why had she left home without permission? Why had she been so silly as to think she could be a holy hermit in a cave?

"Oh, dearest Lord, help me to get back quickly!" cried Catherine. "And, please do not let my family be too cross!"

Almost as soon as the words were out of her mouth, the little girl knew that the first part of her prayer had been heard. Suddenly the rocky cave was gone, with its vines and bushes growing before the door. The song of the birds, the music of the brook, were replaced by the chatter of humans; and looking about her, Catherine saw that it was late afternoon and that she was standing in front of her father's house. There was the smoke, pouring from the chimney of the shop. There were the boys who were learning the trade of dyeing. There was Stefano's grey cat, drinking milk on the back steps. And there was Stefano himself, running eagerly toward her.

"Why didn't you take me with you to Bonaventura's house?" he cried. "It was mean of you to go alone."

"But I didn't go to Bonaventura's. I went to be a hermit," said Catherine. "You must not tell anyone, Stefano. I have had the most wonderful day! I went out in the country and found a cave. Our Lord spoke to me. And then angels carried me home through the air so I would not be late for supper."

Stefano stared at his little sister. "How could a girl like you walk out in the country? You are much too small. And angels don't carry people through the air, Catherine. You know they don't."

"They carried me," said Catherine. "It was like riding on the back of the wind, I came so fast. How I wish you could have been with me, Stefano! It was so beautiful out there in the cave, and I felt that God was so close."

Stefano shrugged his shoulders. Catherine made up such stories. You never knew when to believe her.

"Let's go and eat," he said.

Late that night Catherine lay in her little bed thinking over what had happened, and how it was not God's Will that she should leave home to be a holy person.

"How much I want to serve Him!" she thought. "How much I should have liked to be His little hermit in a cave!"

And as she lay there thinking, she made up her mind. She decided that she would be a holy person right in her own house; that she would be God's little servant in the midst of all the hustle and bustle of her own family.

"For ever and ever I will love Him and serve Him wherever He wants me to," she said. Then she fell asleep, her hair spread like a golden cloud over her pillow.

Nearby hovered a guardian angel, chosen from all eternity to watch over the dyer's little daughter. And the angel smiled as he saw Catherine sleeping, for well he knew that her name would be famous one day all over the world, that many people would journey to see the house wherein she had lived, and that she herself would go on many wonderful journeys in just a few years.

CHAPTER 3

CATHERINE'S HAIR

ATHERINE CONTINUED to live quietly in her father's house, but she never forgot the vision she had seen while out walking with Stefano. Nor could she forget the day she had run away to be a hermit, and the strange power which had brought her swiftly home again when evening drew near. Many times her parents scolded her for spending so much time thinking about the past.

"Why don't you think about us for a change?" her mother would cry. "Don't you know that you are getting to be a big girl now, and that soon it will be time for you to get married?"

"You must try and fix yourself up a bit," said her father. "Then some nice rich man will ask you to be his wife, and his money will help me out in the business."

Poor Catherine! She did not know what to say. No one seemed to understand that she had really seen Our Lord, and had given her heart to Him. How could she get married and promise to love a

"IF YOU DON'T WANT TO GET MARRIED,
CUT OFF YOUR HAIR."

young man when all the time she wanted to live alone so she could always think about God?

Catherine had a stepbrother who was a Dominican priest. His name was Father Thomas della Fonte, and Catherine's parents had adopted him when he was just a little boy. Catherine herself was fond of Father Thomas. One day she went to him with her problem.

"If you don't want to get married, cut off your hair," Father Thomas told her. "No one will bother you then. I, myself, know of no man who would want to marry a girl without any hair."

Catherine was startled. What a perfectly wonderful idea! Why hadn't she thought of it before?

"I'll cut it right off to the roots!" she said. "Oh, thank you so much, Father Thomas!"

Father Thomas shook his head. "There's bound to be a terrible fuss," he warned. "Mother will be furious."

Twelve-year-old Catherine nodded. "I know. But at least they will leave me alone and not bother me about getting dressed up so some rich man will like me. Oh, Father Thomas, if you only knew how I long to be alone!"

The latter sighed. He wished Catherine did not have such strange ideas. Why, for instance, could she not be like her sister Bonaventura? Bonaventura was very happy with her husband and family. She was a good girl and went regularly to church and the Sacraments, and she never caused any trouble by having odd ideas.

"You're not really going to do it," he said, a little

fearfully. "You are only fooling."

Catherine stood up, very tall and straight. "Oh, but I'm not fooling. I'm going to get the scissors right now."

And so it came about. When Catherine's mother discovered that the beautiful golden curls had been cut off, she was furious. She cried and screamed and ran about the house in a great rage.

"What did I ever do to have such a wicked child?" she sobbed. "That Catherine is a fool. No man will ever have her now!"

Jacopo, the patient head of the house, was very upset, too. He took one look at his little daughter's cropped head and then disappeared into his shop, muttering to himself. But the sisters and brothers, including Stefano, thought it all a good joke. Some of them even wondered if their youngest sister were not crazy. Why, in the whole town there was not one girl who would ever be so foolish as to cut off her hair.

"Poor child, perhaps she is losing her mind!" thought poor Jacopo. "May God have mercy on us all!"

"She's a wicked girl!" screamed her mother. "And she must be well punished for being such a nuisance!"

Now, there was a servant girl in Jacopo's household who took care of the hard work. She scrubbed floors, baked the bread, tended to the washing, and hardly ever had a minute to herself. She got up very early in the morning, and when night came she was still hard at work, for there were many tasks in such

SHE SCRUBBED FLOORS, BAKED THE BREAD,
TENDED TO THE WASHING.

a big household. Yet as she was a strong young person, the hard work did not bother her too much.

"Well, I am going to dismiss our maid. Catherine can do the work instead," declared Jacopo's angry wife one morning. "Maybe that will teach her not to be so fussy about having her own way. Maybe in the end she will wish she had a good husband to look after her. Cutting off her hair, indeed! Why, it was the only pretty thing about her!"

So poor Catherine had to be a servant, even though she was only twelve years old. There was no time now for going to Mass in the morning, for prayers in the afternoon, for quiet hours by herself. Her little room was taken away from her and she had no place where she could go to think about God. But no one heard her complain about the new state of affairs. Indeed, Catherine was not too unhappy, for she had decided on a very wonderful plan. She would think of her father as Saint Joseph, her mother as the Blessed Virgin, her numerous brothers and sisters as the disciples of Our Lord. All the work she did about the house would be done for them.

"Dearest Lord, I hope You are pleased with this idea," she said. "It is the best I can think of right now."

Catherine's mother continued to be unkind, finding fault with the way the floor was scrubbed, the bread baked, the clothes washed. But Jacopo was not inclined to hold a grudge for so long. Often he wondered if it were not sinful for his family to be so hard on Catherine, to deprive her of her own room and give her all the unpleasant tasks to do about the house.

"Perhaps she has been punished long enough," he thought, and often made a move to speak to his wife about the matter. But Jacopo was a quiet soul and did not like arguments. The days passed and he kept his peace.

CHAPTER 4

MORE SAINTS IN THE SKY

BUT THERE came a day when Jacopo found himself forced to act. By chance he entered Stefano's room one morning and found Catherine there, kneeling in prayer. Fluttering over her head was a beautiful white dove, while all about her shone a strange light. As the astonished man stared at the sight, the bird flew out the window. Almost at once Catherine scrambled to her feet, sensing that someone had come into the room.

"What bird was that?" asked Jacopo, much upset by what he had seen.

Catherine lowered her eyes, afraid of a scolding because she had taken a few minutes off from her kitchen tasks.

"Father, I didn't see any bird," she said. "I was only thinking about the Most Blessed Trinity."

Jacopo rubbed his hands together nervously. He was a pious man and he had a feeling that he had seen something akin to a miracle. For was not the Holy Ghost often shown in paintings as a white dove? And was there not a strange radiance on

Catherine's face, as though she had really been seeing heavenly things?

"There was a white dove over your head when
I came in," he said. "It is strange that a bird should
enter this house."

After a few minutes he bade Catherine go back
to her duties, but his mind was made up. This child
was certainly different from his other sons and
daughters, but what of it? Perhaps it was true that
God had marked her out for another life than that
of marriage to the young man he had chosen for
her. Perhaps he, Jacopo, was the father of a saint!
What folly, then, to treat this little one as a servant,
to allow her to be scolded and ill-used by everyone!

"There shall be no more of this!" he told himself.
"This is my house. Catherine shall have her rightful
place. If she wishes to remain single, to dress simply, to pray to God in a little room of her own, that
is her business. No one shall interfere."

So presently Catherine was told that she was for-
given and might return to her former position in
the family. No one teased her anymore about having
cut off her hair. No one told her she should think
of finding a husband. For once the girl was left in
peace. Her heart was full of gratitude.

One night, not long after she had been given
back her own room, Catherine was kneeling by her
bed saying her prayers. Suddenly, to her great
amazement, the darkened sky outside her window
became bright with a strange light. A great crowd
of people seemed to be standing in midair, clothed
in the habits of many religious Orders.

"Oh, what a beautiful sight!" cried Catherine. "Saints in the sky again, only ever so many more this time than when I was a little girl!"

And, as she watched, the holy people drew nearer to her window. There was Saint Benedict, with a long white beard and dressed in the somber black of his religious family. Near him was Saint Francis of Assisi, the little poor man who had braved such hardships for Christ. Then came Saint Augustine, Saint Norbert, Saint Bernard, Saint Dominic and a great many other holy men and women who had founded religious Orders. Catherine saw each one of them beckon to her.

"Whatever can they want?" she thought, her heart pounding with excitement.

And then suddenly she saw that Saint Dominic, dressed in a white habit with a black cloak, was coming toward her. In one hand he held a lovely white lily, and in the other the habit of his Order.

"Do not be afraid, Catherine," he said. His voice was wonderfully kind. "Some day you will wear this habit, too."

And then, as though someone had given a signal, all the saints vanished. Once more the little girl was alone, staring out at the dark sky with its few twinkling stars.

Catherine put her head down on the window ledge. What did it all mean? Why had God let her see saints in the sky for a second time? And why had Saint Dominic spoken as he did? Did it mean that she was to be a Dominican nun? Was she to go away from her little room, her big family?

"But I don't think I am meant to live in a convent," she told herself. "Although I shall never marry, because I want to belong completely to God, I don't think He wants me to be a nun. And yet..."

Catherine's eyes lifted once more to the starry skies outside her window. Just what was it that Our Lord wanted of her? Just what kind of a life would she lead when she was grown up?

CHAPTER 5

THE RING

FOUR YEARS passed, and still Catherine did not know what were God's plans for her. Then one day, when she was sixteen years old, she believed she had found out. Her life's work was to pray for sinners who could not be bothered about doing it for themselves. Her life's work was to suffer for them and their sins, so that they would come back to God and He would not have to send them to Hell, where they belonged, but could let them into Heaven with the rest of His children.

"If I could have another room, Mother, the smallest we have, I should be very glad," said Catherine that same day. "You see, I intend to stay there for the rest of my life. I want to pray for the conversion of sinners."

"Are you mad?" cried Lapa, but she did not dare refuse Catherine what she asked. Long ago Jacopo had given orders that the girl was not to be teased or scolded. The good man had never forgotten the time he had seen the white dove fluttering over his daughter's head—the white dove that he felt had been no other than the Holy Ghost.

"Our Catherine is a good girl," he had told his wife more than once. "But she is not like our other children. We must let her alone when we do not understand her."

So Catherine was allowed to have the smallest room in the house for her very own. There was not much in this tiny chamber, with its cold stone floor and the little window that let in only a few streaks of daylight. Her brothers and sisters could not understand how she expected to live there for good, and they were horrified when they learned she intended to sleep on some old boards instead of in a regular bed.

"Even prisoners in jail have a better bed than yours," they said. "Come on, Catherine. Let us help you fix up your room so it will at least be comfortable."

But Catherine would not listen. She had decided to lead a new kind of life where suffering would have a large place. For how else could she expect to save sinners? No, her own comfort must be a thing of the past. No longer would she eat three good meals a day. No longer would she go about her beloved Siena, seeing the trees and the hills and the beautiful churches. The only time she would leave her room would be to go to Mass and the Sacraments.

"Sinners will no longer suffer for their sins," she told her adopted brother, Father Thomas della Fonte, "so I am going to do it for them. Perhaps

God will look at me and feel sorry for those poor people. Perhaps my little pains will merit Heaven for them."

Catherine had been living in her little room for several weeks, seeing no one and eating the small amount of food brought to her, when a new thought entered her mind.

"I want to be a Dominican," she announced. "Not a nun in a convent, but a Dominican Tertiary."

"Why can't you be like other people?" sighed her mother, when she heard the news. Lapa knew that Tertiaries were very holy people, men and women, who wore the habit of a friar or a nun and yet lived in their own homes. Usually they were middle-aged folk, not sixteen-year-old girls like Catherine.

Catherine wondered if her mother were going to be angry. "I think God wants me to be a Tertiary, not a nun," she said. "It is really a wonderful thing to be called to be a Tertiary, Mother."

Lapa shook her head. "Why do you want to dress like a nun and yet not really be one? Oh, Catherine, you are always causing me trouble! First you must cut off your hair. Then you must live in the worst room in the house. Now you want to go and be a Dominican Tertiary! Oh, dear! I never had such trouble with my other children!"

"I have promised not to leave my little room," said Catherine. "Please, Mother, go to the Dominican Tertiaries and tell them I want to be a Tertiary, too."

Lapa shrugged her shoulders. "I will not," she said. "I have no use for being different from other people. Besides, the Tertiaries will never have you. They are all older women—widows, too. They would not want to take in a young girl."

"Oh, please go and ask them!" begged Catherine. "If you only knew how much I want to wear the blessed habit of Saint Dominic!"

"There is no use arguing about it," said Lapa. "I will not have you in my house, wearing a religious habit and looking like a nun. Don't bother me again."

Catherine knelt down in the middle of her little room. She was very sad. How could she go to become a Tertiary when she had promised to remain at home to pray for sinners?

"Dearest Saint Dominic, you will have to help me," she said. And then a little of her sadness left her when she offered her disappointment for the conversion of a certain man who had sworn he would never go to church again.

The same year that Catherine was sixteen, a smallpox plague swept through the town. The dyer's young daughter caught the terrible disease and for a time it seemed as though she would die of it. She lay on her hard bed, her face and body covered with sores, her thoughts far away from this world. Poor Lapa was terribly worried.

"Oh, dear! Isn't there something you would like, Catherine? Perhaps I could make you a pudding or something. Or maybe you would like a little fruit..."

But Catherine shook her head. "The only thing I want is to be a Dominican Tertiary," she said sadly.

Lapa realized that she could hold out no longer. "All right," she said. "I will go to the woman in charge of the Tertiaries and see what can be done."

Lapa's first visit was not a success. The Tertiaries did not want Catherine in their midst. A second and third time the distressed mother told them Catherine would die if they did not come to see her.

"But we do not take young girls for members," said the Tertiaries. "Because we do not live in a convent, we have to be very certain that our Sisters can be trusted. Who can be sure that your Catherine would not disgrace us?"

Lapa's temper began to rise. "My girl is as good as any of you!" she cried. "And if you do not come to see her and give her the habit, she will die and you will be no better than murderers! So there!"

Most of the Tertiaries were grey-haired ladies, and for a long time they talked about the dyer's daughter. They had heard about the time she had cut off her hair and how she had shut herself up in a small room to pray for sinners.

"She is a queer one," they said. "We had better not have anything to do with her." Yet some of them were worried. Supposing the girl really did deserve to become a daughter of Saint Dominic?

"Oh, it will not hurt to take a look at her," said one. "We don't have to give her the habit if we don't want to."

So all the grey-haired ladies went to Jacopo's house to visit Catherine. They went through the big front door and up a winding stairway until they

THEY CAME TO THE POOR LITTLE ROOM
WHERE CATHERINE LAY SICK.

came to the poor little room where Catherine lay sick. When they saw her, so white and thin, so resigned to God's Will, so anxious to be a Dominican like themselves, they changed their minds. They had been afraid that Jacopo's daughter was beautiful, and interested only in pretty clothes and in having a good time.

"Why, you are really homely!" said one Tertiary, looking at Catherine's face that was all marked up with smallpox sores. "I guess you never thought about getting married, did you?"

Catherine slowly shook her head, her eyes upon the lovely black and white habits the Tertiaries wore. Oh, if only she, too, could be Saint Dominic's child, his little daughter working for God in the midst of the world!

"I have no love but Our Lord," she said simply.

When the Tertiaries left Catherine, they told her mother that they had changed their minds. As soon as the girl was well enough, she might come to the church and receive the Dominican habit.

"She seems a good girl," said the lady in charge of the Tertiaries. "If she behaves herself, we are willing to have her one of us."

Lapa bowed stiffly. She did not like these ladies at all.

When Catherine heard that she was to receive the Dominican habit, that she was to be a religious with the whole world for her convent, she cried for joy. In no time at all she was well again and able to go to the church for the ceremony. When she returned home in her new outfit, a white wool dress with a black cape and a white veil on her head, her mother shook her head sadly.

"You look just like a nun," she mourned. "You are no longer my little girl. Oh, Catherine, why did you have to do it?"

Catherine's eyes glowed. "Because it is my vocation," she said. "And someday it will be yours, too, Mother. Someday you will be a Dominican Tertiary yourself."

Lapa's temper began to rise again. "I wouldn't be seen dead in an outfit like that!" she cried. Catherine did not answer. She was too happy for another argument.

After receiving the Dominican habit, Catherine set about praying for sinners more than ever. She locked herself in her small room and never left it, except to go to church. She learned to sleep on her hard wooden bed, remembering that Our Lord had died for her on the hard wood of the Cross; and if she ever grew tired of the bread and water and vegetables her mother brought to the door, she never said so.

"I am not really worth much to my family," she said to herself. "All I can do is to suffer a little for sinners. Oh, dearest Lord, teach me how to suffer well!"

Now, although Catherine did not ask for many pleasures, there was one favor she wanted very much indeed, and this was to be able to read. Children in those days, particularly girls, did not go to school, and so Jacopo's sixteen-year-old daughter had never learned to read or write at all. She could not even make out one word in the Bible, and when the Dominican priests chanted their prayers in church, she could not follow them.

"Dear Lord, I am awfully stupid," she said one day. "Won't You please help me, so I can read prayers?"

When Catherine asked for this favor, Our Lord was pleased. He waited until she picked up a paper that had some writing on it, and then He suddenly flooded her mind with a bright light. In one second He let her learn how to read even the hardest books. A little later, He showed her how to write.

"Oh, this is wonderful!" cried the young girl. "Now I shall be able to learn so much about You, dearest Lord. Thank You!"

There were plenty of times when Catherine grew very lonely in her little room, even if she could read books. Then it was that the devil would come and tempt her to forget all about praying for sinners.

"It is all a waste of time," he would say. "Look at other girls of your age. They are out enjoying themselves. They are wearing pretty clothes and going to parties. You are silly to stay in this dark room and say so many prayers. Soon you will be an ugly old woman, and no one will care whether you are alive or dead. God does not care two straws about you," laughed the evil one. "Otherwise why would He let me torment you?"

Catherine was bothered almost every day by such talk from the devil. But she knew that as long as God loved her and she loved God, nothing else mattered. She did not enter into arguments with the tempter, but just kept on with her prayers and penances.

After Catherine had rejected the devil's lies, Our Lord came to comfort her. He told her that He was well pleased with her faithfulness to Him. Also, she was saving many sinners by her prayers and loneliness. Why, there was a great crowd of them already in Heaven, waiting to thank her for what she had done!

"You are very dear to Me," He told her one night. "And I am going to give you a little reward."

It was the night before Ash Wednesday of the third year that Catherine had stayed in her little room almost as a prisoner. She was nineteen years old now.

"What are You going to give me, dear Lord?" asked Catherine.

And then she saw that Our Lord had brought a great many holy people with Him. There was the Blessed Virgin, Saint John the Evangelist, Saint Paul, the prophet David and her own spiritual father, Saint Dominic. It made quite a crowd in her little room.

Presently the Blessed Virgin came toward the wondering Catherine. "Give me your hand, Catherine," she said. Catherine put out her right hand and the Blessed Mother put it into the hand of her Son. The prophet David began to play sweet music on his little harp and all the saints gathered close to see what would happen.

"I take you for My own chosen one," said Our Lord, and then He placed on Catherine's finger a wonderful golden ring. It had four beautiful stones set about a diamond, and it was certainly the loveliest ring that Catherine had ever seen.

"You will wear this in remembrance of My love for the rest of your life," said Our Lord. And then He added: "But it will always be invisible to other people."

The prophet David played happy music on his harp, the Blessed Virgin and her company of saints smiled, and Catherine was beside herself with joy. The whole ceremony had been just like a wedding.

"Oh, thank You!" was all she could say. "Thank You very much!"

CHAPTER 6

THE LEPER WOMAN AND THE STUBBORN YOUNG CRIMINAL

I T WAS only a few days after He had given her the beautiful ring that Our Lord appeared to Catherine again.

"Three years you have been living in your little room," He said. "In that time you have saved many sinners from Hell by your prayers and sufferings. But now, your time for hiding is over. You must go back to live with your family."

Catherine could hardly believe her ears. "Oh, but dear Lord, I don't want to go back into the world. You know that I hate the world!"

"But I have work for you to do outside this room. Come, My daughter, go down to dinner today and tell your mother the news."

Poor Catherine was in despair. Yet if Our Lord wanted her to go back into the world. . .

"Yes, dear Lord," she said. "I will go."

When she unlocked her door, smoothed out her white Tertiary habit and came downstairs, her family was overcome with surprise. It was just as though Catherine had been dead and then had suddenly walked in and said "Boo!"

"What is the matter?" asked everyone. "We thought you had locked yourself up for good."

"Oh, she is only tired of being holy," said one of the brothers. "It is always like that with girls."

Lapa eyed Catherine anxiously. "Are you sick?" she asked. "Would you like a good meal for a change?"

Catherine smiled and shook her head. "I am all right," she said. "And I am not tired of loving God. I have only come back to you because He has told me to do so."

Somebody laughed. Catherine was still strange, as strange as the day when she had cut off her golden curls and promised she would never marry.

"What can somebody like you do?" they wanted to know.

Catherine looked at her beautiful invisible ring and tried not to cry. Oh, it was going to be very hard to live in the family again! In the last few years several of her brothers had married and had brought their wives home to live with them. Although Jacopo's house was still as big as ever, there seemed to be people everywhere.

"I just want to be your servant," she said simply. "I can wash and cook and mend a little. Please let me be of help!"

So into the big family of Jacopo, the dyer, came nineteen-year-old Catherine. From the start her days were spent in working for her family, but she also went out to help the sick and poor. With her father's permission, she took them food and clothes and money. One of her special charges was an old woman called Thecca, whom no one else would bother with because she had a bad case of leprosy.

"Poor Thecca has no one to look after her," thought Catherine. "They are going to send her away from the hospital to the leper-house outside the city."

It was true that the skin from Thecca's body was almost eaten away by the dreadful disease. Indeed, Thecca's body was little more than rotting bones.

"But God loves Thecca, and so I will love her, too," Catherine thought. Each morning and evening, she went the long distance to visit Thecca in the hospital. Thecca was allowed to stay there since Catherine had offered to care for her. In a basket Catherine carried food, water and clean bandages, and her heart was truly happy that she was able to help someone at last. Had not Our Lord often told her that what one did for the poor was done for Him, too? Catherine cared for Thecca with as much kindness as if she had been her own mother.

But, seeing that Catherine continued to be so good to her, Thecca became ungrateful and began to treat Catherine as her slave. She even spoke insulting words to her. Most people would have gone home in a great hurry.

"Poor old soul!" thought Catherine. "This is what can happen when one is sick of a terrible disease." And she pretended not to hear the mean things Thecca said. She swept the little hut as it had never been swept before. She cleaned the dreadful sores on the old woman's body, prepared a tasty meal and waited on her just as though she were a queen.

"You shall catch leprosy, too!" cried Lapa when Catherine came home each night. "Why can't you leave that ungrateful old woman alone?"

To test Catherine, God allowed her to catch leprosy. Her hands began to have little sores on them. But Catherine kept on caring for Thecca. She felt that Thecca would not live much longer and she wanted to help her as much as possible. She wanted to help her die a good death. For herself, what did anything matter? If she had caught leprosy, she would have a little more suffering to offer for sinners.

And then came the day when Thecca died. Catherine assisted her up to her last moment, praying and urging Thecca to pray. No one but Catherine was in the poor little hut. It was she who washed and clothed the rotten old body and then buried it in the grave.

"May she rest in peace, and may she pray for me!" Catherine thought, as she finished her task. "Certainly the poor old woman suffered much on earth."

But while she was standing by Thecca's grave, Catherine happened to glance down at her own hands. Wonder of wonders! The leprosy was gone. The sores that had been troubling them for weeks, the dreadful sores that could grow and spread until they covered one's entire body, had disappeared.

"Oh, dear Lord, how good You are to me!" she

thought. "Now I need not worry about giving leprosy to those at home."

Besides caring for Thecca and another cross old woman called Andrea, Catherine kept busy with many other duties. One of her favorite tasks was to go to the prisons and try to comfort the men and women who had been placed there for their crimes. One young man in particular claimed Catherine's devotion, for she knew he had been sentenced to death and had never repented of his sin. He was a murderer. Not many girls of Catherine's age would have been brave enough to talk with him.

"Why won't you go to confession?" she asked him kindly one day. "You know you have only a little while longer to live."

At these words the young man began to curse and swear in a dreadful fashion. "I am going to Hell! Don't try to stop me!" he said. "I have been so wicked all my life that there is no use in asking God to forgive me."

Catherine's loving heart was torn. "If you had committed every sin in the whole world, God would still want you to come to Him and be sorry," she reminded him. "God can forgive anything, if we only ask Him."

For days Catherine talked like this to the young man. She offered many, many prayers and sacrifices for him. Finally he began to believe her. "All right. Bring me a priest and I'll go to confession," he said. "I don't really want to go to Hell, you know."

Catherine brought a priest to the prison and the

young man received the Sacrament of Penance. Afterwards, Catherine knew that his soul was all beautiful with Sanctifying Grace. Sometimes God even showed Catherine the great beauty of a soul in the State of Grace, and Catherine would go into rapture for joy.

When the time came for the criminal to die on the gallows, none of his friends or relatives came to say good-bye. Only Catherine was there. It was she who walked with him to his death, helping him to say little prayers and telling him to trust in God's sweet mercy. Some of the strangers around laughed at the sight of the young Tertiary, in her black and white habit, comforting a hardened criminal.

"Who is she?" they asked. "What is she doing up there with a criminal?"

"Oh, she is the daughter of Jacopo, the dyer," was the answer. "She is always with the poor and friendless."

Catherine did not care how many people laughed at her. She knew she had helped save a soul. She would even have been glad to die in order to save a soul.

Catherine's dear father, Jacopo, was now an old man. He was dying and did not have long to live. Catherine did not want her father to have to suffer in Purgatory after he died, so she asked Our Lord to let him go straight to Heaven. "Dear Lord," she prayed, "if it is necessary, I will bear the pains my father should have suffered."

At the moment when Jacopo died, Catherine felt a sharp pain in her side. It was to stay with her

"SHE IS ALWAYS WITH THE POOR AND FRIENDLESS."

the rest of her life. But the pain always gave Catherine joy, for she knew it meant that God had taken her dear father to Heaven.

CHAPTER 7

PLANS FOR A LONG JOURNEY

TODAY, as we all know, the Holy Father lives in Rome. Rome is the Eternal City, and if we want to visit the Pope we must go there to see him. But in Catherine's day it was different. Because of various political troubles in Europe, the Popes had made France their home for many years. They had chosen a pretty little French city called Avignon as their headquarters, and most of them had never even been to Italy or seen their proper home in the Vatican.

"It's too bad that the Pope lives in France," said many people. "If he were in Rome, where he ought to be, how much better things would be for the Church!"

Catherine knew that the Holy Father, Pope Gregory the Eleventh, liked living in France, where the climate was pleasant and he had many friends. But she felt sure he would come to Rome if only he understood how much he was needed. From the East there was danger of invasion by the Turks, who hated all Christians and would be only too glad to blot them off the face of the earth.

"Someone ought to go to Avignon to tell the Pope about it," she thought. Often she prayed that a strong man would rise up to defend the Church in her hour of need. But no strong man appeared, and matters went from bad to worse. Catherine continued to live in her father's big house, helping with the work there and visiting the poor and sick when she had a little free time. She was still very much in love with Our Lord. When she looked at His beautiful ring on her finger, she would pray that He would make of her a little tool with which He might do His work.

Were there sinners to be met? "Let me meet them," she prayed. "And put wise words into my mouth so that I may bring them to You."

Were there people who would not say any prayers, who would not do penance for their sins? "Let me suffer for them," begged Catherine. "Let me help get them into Heaven."

Although Our Lord loved Catherine, too, and showed Himself to her very often, He also allowed her to suffer for sinners. Because He Himself had died on the Cross, with cruel nails in His Hands and Feet, He let Catherine know something of the pain He had known. One day when she was twenty-eight years old and on a visit to the city of Pisa, He pierced her hands, feet and side with wounds like He Himself had borne. For the rest of her life Catherine felt as though she, too, had been crucified, but there were not many people who knew of her sufferings. Like the beautiful ring, the wounds of the Crucifixion remained invisible on Catherine's body. But people did know that Jacopo's young daughter was different from themselves. They watched her when she received Holy Communion and saw that almost at once she seemed to faint away in a kind of trance. Sometimes it would be two or three hours before she was herself again. They knew, too, that Catherine did not eat or drink like ordinary folk. When Our Lord came to her in the Blessed Eucharist she received all the strength she needed.

Poor Lapa used to worry about her young daughter, who wore the black and white habit of Saint Dominic's family and yet was not a nun.

"What is ever going to happen to her?" she often asked Father Thomas della Fonte, her adopted son. "She will not eat or drink. She goes around with the most peculiar kind of people. She prays and prays and prays. And she hardly ever sleeps in that hard bed of hers!"

It was also a fact that people followed Catherine wherever she went. They knew she was a saint. She had a special spiritual charm about her, and people loved to be near her. These people were Catherine's spiritual family.

But many sinners also came to Catherine. With great kindness she would tell them about God's merciful love and urge them to repent. Often several priests had to go wherever Catherine went, to hear confessions for hours and hours.

Father Thomas would try to comfort his worried

mother, but deep in his heart he was troubled. It
was not enough that his little sister should pray and
suffer for the sinners she loved. It was not enough
that she had established a small group of men and
women whom she encouraged to help her in her
different works. The latest plan—and he dreaded
to make it known to Lapa—was that Catherine had
decided to go to see the Pope. She had made up
her mind to make the long journey to France, on
foot if need be, to tell the Holy Father that he must
return to his rightful place in Rome.

"Long have I prayed that someone else would do
this," she had informed Father Thomas only
recently, "but seeing that there is no one, I am
ready to go myself."

Catherine at Avignon! Father Thomas hated to
think of it. How could his poor little sister have
courage enough to talk to the Holy Father, to the
Cardinals, and tell them where their duty lay?

"You shouldn't think of going," he had told her
bluntly. "A woman's place is in the home, Catherine. Don't you know you shouldn't try to tell the
Pope what to do?"

But she had refused to listen to him. It was her
duty to talk to the Pope, she had said. Our Lord
had told her so. And nothing would stop her.

CHAPTER 8

CATHERINE GOES TO SEE
THE HOLY FATHER

CATHERINE'S great friend and confessor, Father Raymond of Capua, had gone to Avignon some time before. He was on hand when Catherine herself arrived. It had been a long hard journey, but the young Dominican Tertiary would not take time to rest before seeing Pope Gregory the Eleventh. Dusty and tired as she was, Catherine begged Father Raymond to take her to the Pope at once.

"Oh, he must come to Rome right away!" she cried. "There is a terrible war going on now, with one city fighting against another and people dying by the thousands. No one can make peace but our good Holy Father."

Father Raymond nodded, but his heart was sad. How was a girl like Catherine going to be able to talk to the Pope? Great men were in fear of him, and few if any had ever dared tell him that he should not be living in France. Yet perhaps, through a miracle, Jacopo's daughter Catherine would

53

influence him. Perhaps she might be able to get him to return to Rome. Perhaps he would also make peace among the warring cities.

Catherine prayed and prayed, deep down within her heart, that the Holy Ghost would give her wise and powerful words to say. When she visited the Pope, she said, "If you do not come to Rome, dearest Father, thousands of your people will die." She told Pope Gregory about the wars among the Italian cities, and about the Turks. The Turks were haters of the Catholic religion. They wanted to stamp it out at once by fire and sword.

"You belong in Rome, Most Holy Father," Catherine said. Everyone knew that Rome was the city of Saint Peter, the first Pope.

The Holy Father said yes, he knew, and he was already planning to return to Rome, but he could not go yet. One reason came up, then another, then another, why he could not go just yet. Plus, all his relatives were in France. And it would break the heart of Gregory's dear old father if his son went away to Rome.

The Holy Father needed lots of courage to come to Rome. It would be very hard for him.

So Catherine offered many prayers and sacrifices for him. She wrote letter after letter to the Holy Father and his Cardinals. Long ago Our Lord had taught her how to read and write, and she was now making good use of her skill. She also spoke to the Holy Father in person.

"I have never heard a woman speak so well," he told his Cardinals. And even these wise men had

"I HAVE NEVER HEARD A WOMAN SPEAK SO WELL."

to admit that Catherine was wise, too.

"There is nothing in the Catechism that she does not know," Pope Gregory went on. "She really believes she is doing God's Will by coming here to see me."

But there were plenty of people who tried to poison the Pope's mind about Catherine. Some said she was a wicked woman. Others insisted that she was only trying to make trouble and had set herself up as leader because she was full of pride.

"Don't believe a word she tells you," they said to the Holy Father. "She is only an ignorant girl."

The Pope did not know what to think, and many times he wished he had never heard of Catherine.

Then one morning, after about six months, the Holy Father called Catherine to him. He was dressed in a wonderful white robe, with a cross of gold hung about his neck. All about him were Cardinals and princes in scarlet robes and cloaks of ermine. Catherine, in her poor Tertiary habit, came in before the great throne and knelt down before Saint Peter's successor on earth. Her heart was beating very fast. Oh, what was to be the result of her visit?

The Pope, seeing her anxiety, smiled a little.

"My Daughter," he said, "how old are you?"

The question surprised Catherine. She answered simply that she had spent twenty-nine years on earth, trying to save her soul.

"Twenty-nine years," mused Pope Gregory. "That is not very old. Why, you have spoken to me many times without fear, boldly urging me to take action."

Some of the princes and nobles were smiling among themselves, but Catherine paid no attention. "Most Holy Father, it is not I who urged you, but God," she said, looking into the kindly eyes of the Pope.

For a while Pope Gregory held the golden cross about his neck and seemed to be lost in thought. But suddenly he beckoned to the anxious girl at his feet.

"I have heard that you have worked miracles," he said. "In Siena they tell many wonderful things about you. But there is one thing I must know. Will you show me your hands?"

Very slowly Catherine put both her hands before her. She had been afraid of this, that the Pope would ask to see the wounds of Christ's Crucifixion which had been given to her the year before. Oh, how she hoped they would remain invisible, as they always were! There had been enough talk about her in Avignon already.

Although the Pope looked long and hard at Catherine's hands, he could see nothing unusual. Then, as he touched the palms, he saw that Catherine winced.

"Ah . . ." he said. "Then it is true. . .you do have Christ's holy wounds. . ."

Catherine hung her head. "Please, I beg of you, Most Holy Father, do not bother yourself about me," she whispered. "Think instead of Rome, think of your people in Italy. Think of the nobles who will make peace when you come to your rightful place in Rome. Think of the dreadful Turks."

The Holy Father smiled. This girl had truly been sent to him by God.

"Yes," he said. "I will come to Rome soon. I will lead my people."

CHAPTER 9

CATHERINE'S LAST BIG SACRIFICE

WHEN CATHERINE went back to Italy, she was greeted as a heroine. The Holy Father was coming to Rome! She had talked to him, and he had listened to her.

"Oh, you are wonderful after all!" cried her mother, half laughing and half crying. "Perhaps there is something about being a Dominican Tertiary. . ." And then she told Catherine that she had decided to become a Tertiary, too. "If they will have me," she added.

Catherine could not help smiling just a little. She was remembering the terrible fuss that had been made when she had wanted to receive the black and white habit of Saint Dominic. Her mother had scolded and scolded, and yet now. . .

"You shall be received right away," she said. "Oh, Mother, I am so happy that you want to be a Dominican, too!"

Perhaps Catherine thought back to that day, years ago, when Lapa had died. All those present had seen her die. But Catherine knew her mother had not been prepared for death; she had not accepted her approaching death or received the Last Sacraments.

While the others prepared for the funeral, Catherine poured out her heart to Jesus. She reminded Him of promises He had made to her: a promise that no one of her house would go to Hell, and a promise that her mother would not be taken from this world against her own will. Catherine beseeched Our Lord to give back Lapa's life. With great faith she had even prayed, "Lord, I shall not move from here until You have restored my mother to me alive!"

God heard Catherine's fervent prayer. Lapa's body began to move, and she came back to life again. She was to live to be 89 years old.

And so now Lapa became a Tertiary, probably never realizing that centuries later, in an unknown land called the United States of America, there would be thousands of men and women going about their business as Dominican Tertiaries, too. And although they would dress just like other people, and no one would ever guess that they belonged to Saint Dominic's religious family, they would be just as truly members of the Dominican Order as Catherine and herself.

Naturally Catherine was very happy when Pope Gregory left Avignon and came to live at the Vatican in Rome. She was sure that now the enemies of the Church would not have a chance to make any trouble. But alas for her plans! The poor Holy

Father was in Rome only two years when he fell ill and died. And then came trouble, and plenty of it, for some people wanted the next Pope to be an Italian and others said he should be a Frenchman, like Pope Gregory. An election was held and an Italian was declared to be the new Holy Father—Pope Urban the Sixth. But there were plenty of people who said that Pope Urban had not been properly elected and therefore was not Pope at all.

"Let us have another election," said these people, and the first thing anyone knew they had chosen a Frenchman for Pope—Clement the Eighth.

Catherine was sick at the news. How could there be two Popes?

"Urban the Sixth is the real Holy Father," she said.

"Clement the Eighth is the real Holy Father," said thousands of other people, who really believed they were right.

And then there began to be fights everywhere, just as there would be in our own country if, after an election, two men claimed they were President and should live in the White House. Catherine was terribly upset over the whole thing, and many people even blamed all the trouble on her.

"If you had not gone to Avignon, if you had not urged Pope Gregory to come to Rome, there would not be all this mix-up," they said. "Didn't you know the climate in Rome wouldn't agree with him?"

Catherine suffered and prayed over the dreadful state of affairs, and finally decided to leave Siena and go down to Rome to visit Pope Urban the Sixth—the real Holy Father. Perhaps she could do something to help him. A few of her friends went along, too, but none of them was happy. They thought Catherine looked a wreck.

"She will get sick and die if she doesn't look out," they said. "Why, she is nothing but skin and bones!"

When she heard them talking this way, Catherine could only smile wearily. She had long ago offered her life for sinners, her prayers and sufferings for their conversion. Now she had asked Our Lord to take her away entirely, but to give peace to the world instead and settle the matter of the two men both claiming to be Pope. Deep down in her heart she felt He had heard her prayer and that she would die soon.

"But you mustn't say such prayers!" cried her mother, who now wore the habit of a Dominican Tertiary as well as Catherine. "What should we do if you died?"

"You would go on serving God," Catherine said. "And you would do it much better than I have ever done. Oh, Mother, how awful it is to be a failure!"

No doubt Catherine was thinking of how she had brought back Pope Gregory to Rome, only to have him die and the terrible trouble of the two "Popes" come to pass.

"Well, I shall never think of you as a failure," said Lapa. "Really, you have been the best of all my children. Your poor father (God rest his soul) thought so, too." And she tried to comfort her poor daughter as well as she could.

But of course Catherine was not a failure in the most important thing: in loving God and carrying out His holy Will. She had done this her whole life long.

When Catherine went to Rome, Pope Urban was very glad to see her, but it pained him when he heard that she would soon die.

"How do you know this?" he asked. Catherine told him how she had offered her life to God in return for peace in Italy for Church and State.

"Yes, I know He has heard me," she said. "I shall die here in Rome, this very year."

Because soon she was too sick to go to church, Pope Urban allowed Catherine to have an altar in her room where Mass could be said every day. Lying on her poor wooden bed, she would assist at the Holy Sacrifice as well as she could. When she received Holy Communion, her face would light up with a wonderful smile. God was still her only food. When she looked at the beautiful invisible ring on her finger, she knew that He was her only love, too.

As she had foretold, Catherine died in Rome at the age of thirty-three. She never saw the matter settled about the two men claiming to be Pope, but of course we know that it was. Today there is but one Pope and nobody would ever argue about it. And nobody ever argues about Catherine, either. We all know that she is a great Saint, not because she had visions and wonderful favors from God, but because she was not afraid to do whatever God asked of her.

During her life Catherine wrote down some of the things God said to her. These are in a book called the *Dialogue*. This holy book has become very famous.

Saint Catherine of Siena, in Heaven with God today, pray for those who have read this little story of your life!

ST. CATHERINE OF SIENA, IN HEAVEN, PRAY FOR
THOSE WHO HAVE READ THE STORY OF YOUR LIFE.

By the same author...

6 GREAT CATHOLIC BOOKS FOR CHILDREN

...and for all young people ages 10 to 100!!

1137 THE CHILDREN OF FATIMA—And Our Lady's Message to the World. 162 pp. PB. 15 Illus. Impr. The wonderful story of Our Lady's appearances to little Jacinta, Francisco and Lucia at Fatima in 1917.   6.00

1138 THE CURÉ OF ARS—The Story of St. John Vianney, Patron Saint of Parish Priests. 211 pp. PB. 38 Illus. Impr. The many adventures that met young St. John Vianney when he set out to become a priest.   9.00

1139 THE LITTLE FLOWER—The Story of St. Therese of the Child Jesus. 167 pp. PB. 24 Illus. Impr. Tells what happened when little Therese decided to become a saint.   7.00

1140 PATRON SAINT OF FIRST COMMUNICANTS—The Story of Blessed Imelda Lambertini. 85 pp. PB. 14 Illus. Impr. Tells of the wonderful miracle God worked to answer little Imelda's prayer.   4.00

1141 THE MIRACULOUS MEDAL—The Story of Our Lady's Appearances to St. Catherine Labouré. 107 pp. PB. 21 Illus. Impr. The beautiful story of what happened when young Sister Catherine saw Our Lady.   5.00

1142 ST. LOUIS DE MONTFORT—The Story of Our Lady's Slave. 211 pp. PB. 20 Illus. Impr. The remarkable story of the priest who went around helping people become "slaves" of Jesus through Mary.   9.00

1143 ALL 6 BOOKS ABOVE (Reg. 40.00)   THE SET: 32.00

At your Bookdealer or direct from the Publisher.

Also by the same author...

6 <u>MORE</u> GREAT CATHOLIC BOOKS FOR CHILDREN

...and for all young people ages 10 to 100!!

1200 SAINT THOMAS AQUINAS—The Story of "The Dumb Ox." 81 pp. PB. 16 Illus. Impr. The remarkable story of how St. Thomas, called in school "The Dumb Ox," became the greatest Catholic teacher ever.   5.00

1201 SAINT CATHERINE OF SIENA—The Story of the Girl Who Saw Saints in the Sky. 65 pp. PB. 13 Illus. The amazing life of the most famous Catherine in the history of the Church.   4.00

1202 SAINT HYACINTH OF POLAND—The Story of The Apostle of the North. 189 pp. PB. 16 Illus. Impr. Shows how the holy Catholic Faith came to Poland, Lithuania, Prussia, Scandinavia and Russia.   8.00

1203 SAINT MARTIN DE PORRES—The Story of The Little Doctor of Lima, Peru. 122 pp. PB. 16 Illus. Impr. The incredible life and miracles of this black boy who became a great saint.   6.00

1204 SAINT ROSE OF LIMA—The Story of The First Canonized Saint of the Americas. 132 pp. PB. 13 Illus. Impr. The remarkable life of the little Rose of South America.   7.00

1205 PAULINE JARICOT—Foundress of the Living Rosary and The Society for the Propagation of the Faith. 244 pp. PB. 21 Illus. Impr. The story of a rich young girl and her many spiritual adventures.   10.00

1206 ALL 6 BOOKS ABOVE (Reg. 40.00)   THE SET: 32.00

At your Bookdealer or direct from the Publisher.

ORDER FORM

TAN BOOKS AND PUBLISHERS, INC.
P.O. Box 424, Rockford, Illinois 61105
TOLL FREE: 1-800-437-5876
FAX: 1-815-987-1833

Please send me

(Qty.)   (Stock No.)   (Title)   (Amount)

_____ _____ _____ _____

_____ _____ _____ _____

_____ _____ _____ _____

_____ _____ _____ _____

_____ _____ _____ _____

_____ _____ _____ _____

☐ Encl. is payment of _____.   Subtotal _____

☐ Charge to ____ MasterCard ____ VISA   6% Sales Tax _____
                              (Ill. res. only)
           ____ Discover   Post./Hdlg. * _____

Exp. date: Month _____ Year _____   TOTAL _____

Acct. No.: _____

Account Name _____

Signature _____
                 (Do not send us your card.)

Name   _____

Street   _____

City   _____

State _____ Zip _____

U.S. & CAN. POST/HDLG: If total order=$1-$10, add $2.00;
$10.01-$20, add $3.00; $20.01-$30, add $4.00; $30.01-$50, add $5.00;
$50.01-$75, add $6.00; $75.01-up, add $7.00.

MARY FABYAN WINDEATT

Mary Fabyan Windeatt could well be called the "storyteller of the saints," for such indeed she was. And she had a singular talent for bringing out doctrinal truths in her stories, so that without even realizing it, young readers would see the Catholic catechism come to life in the lives of the saints.

Mary Fabyan Windeatt wrote at least 21 books for children, plus the text of about 28 Catholic story coloring books. At one time there were over 175,000 copies of her books on the saints in circulation. She contributed a regular "Children's Page" to the monthly Dominican magazine, *The Torch*.

Miss Windeatt began her career of writing for the Catholic press around age 24. After graduating from San Diego State College in 1934, she had gone to New York looking for work in advertising. Not finding any, she sent a story to a Catholic magazine. It was accepted—and she continued to write. Eventually Miss Windeatt wrote for 33 magazines, contributing verse, articles, book reviews and short stories.

Having been born in 1910 in Regina, Saskatchewan, Canada, Mary Fabyan Windeatt received the Licentiate of Music degree from Mount Saint Vincent College in Halifax, Nova Scotia at age 17. With her family she moved to San Diego in that same year, 1927. In 1940 Miss Windeatt received an A.M. degree from Columbia University. Later, she lived with her mother near St. Meinrad's Abbey, St. Meinrad, Indiana. Mary Fabyan Windeatt died on November 20, 1979.

(Much of the above information is from Catholic Authors: Contemporary Biographical Sketches 1930-1947, *ed. by Matthew Hoehn, O.S.B., B.L.S., St. Mary's Abbey, Newark, N.J., 1957.)*